# Get Comfortable Being Uncomfortable
## Improving Your Performance

# Bob Molle

*Get Comfortable Being Uncomfortable*
Copyright © 2011 by Robert Molle. All rights reserved.

No part of this book may be used or reproduced in any manner whatsoever without the prior written permission of the publisher, except in the case of brief quotations embodied in reviews.

Bob Molle's books may be purchased for educational, business, or sales promotional use from his website at www.bobmolle.com

Edited by:
David Wilson
Helena Bachmann
Karen Molle

I dedicate this book to my family. First and foremost, my parents for never losing faith in me even though I probably drove you crazy. Next, to my children Ryan, Sarah and Sean, thanks for allowing your Daddy Man to be part of your exciting experiences. Finally, to my wife Karen, we all appreciate everything you do for us, but sometimes we forget to say it.

# Introduction

"Do you want to improve your performance?"

I've asked this question to crowds of people in countless places over the years, and not one person has ever failed to raise their hand. I have met so many frustrated and disillusioned people who, despite their best efforts, have had limited – or no – success achieving their goals. Not surprisingly, the question that is asked most often by people coming up to me after my seminars is: "How can I stay motivated?"

These folks have set solid goals for themselves, so it's not as though they are floating through life aimlessly. They want to achieve personal and professional successes. They want to be happy.

So why is it that many of their goals are so difficult to reach?

I believe that while our objectives may be very good, the goal-setting process we follow is flawed. The reason why so few people manage to realize their dreams is that they focus on the *how* rather than the *why*. With the right resources, anyone can figure out how to do something. The more important thing to consider is *why* you want to do it.

For example, everyone would like to get in better shape. Everyone also knows that the way to do this is improving your exercise and diet. This is the easy part. The most difficult part is staying committed to your goal by knowing *why* you're doing it.

Through self-examination, you might determine the reason you're doing it is to look better with your shirt off. In another case, someone might be doing it to lose weight so they can lower their risk of heart disease, which has been plaguing their family for years. It doesn't matter if your reason is for vanity or as serious as life or death, what matters is whether or not the *why* is strong enough for you to perservere.

If you can determine the answer to that question, and find your *why,* you will be able to persist through the difficult times and stay on track. In other words, it is not only about getting where you want to go, but even more importantly, knowing *why* you want to get there in the first place.

Finding your *why* is not a one-time process. After all, life is not static; it is constantly evolving and changing our moment-by-moment perceptions, priorities, and goals. Therefore, we must continually re-evaluate what we want to accomplish, and *why* it matters to us.

These moments of evaluation will make you uncomfortable; at least they should. When we are honest with ourselves, we often realize that we must change course into the unknown, and do things that will not be easy. This is why it's crucial to learn the art of "getting comfortable being uncomfortable."

This book is a collection of stories and reflections about people that have inspired and guided me to success through all the stages of my life – athletics, coaching, business, speaking, and most recently, writing. All of the experiences described in this book will hopefully provide inspiration in your own journey to leaving your comfort zone and finding the answers to all of life's *whys*.

*Some people hear their own inner voices with great clearness.
And they live by what they hear. Such people become crazy...
or they become legend.*

-Jim Harrison

# The Recovery

It was the summer of 1984 and I had made the Canadian Olympic wrestling team. I was excited to get ready for the event I had dreamed about and worked toward for many years. The team wanted me to be prepared to take on men of any size, so they brought in the biggest man they could find to help me train. His name was John Tenta and, at the time, he was the World Junior Champion. John later transitioned his career to professional wrestling and was known by the stage name "The Earthquake." The earth probably did shake under him: he was 6 feet 7 inches tall and weighed close to 400 pounds.

Leading up to the Olympics, the team trained twice a day. Because I was only 21 at the time, my back hadn't gotten used to wrestling with a hulk of a man like John. My back was getting tighter and sorer every day. The ice treatments and massages were having very little impact on my stiffness. But being as the Olympics were only a few weeks away, I certainly didn't want to miss practice.

One morning I awoke to go to practice and I could barely get out of bed. I was bent over to one side and could not walk. I was thinking I would have to take off a couple of days for sure and get the back treated, or, at the very least straightened out by a chiropractor. This was my plan, but my back seemed to get progressively worse each day. I now had numbness and shooting pain along the side of my leg. It was clearly time to see a doctor.

After consulting every specialist I could find, the unanimous diagnosis was that I had a major disc problem. Further tests indicated that one of my discs had ruptured and surgery was the only option.

I could not believe it. How could this be happening to me? This was my Olympic dream. This was not the way I scripted my story! There was no way I could compete in the Olympics now. It was already July and the games would be starting in Los Angeles in a matter of weeks. Even if I could have the surgery quickly, my recovery would take months, not weeks. I buried my head in my pillow and balled my eyes out for hours. My dream was dead.

My pain finally reached a point where I couldn't walk anymore. I was admitted to the hospital under the care of a neurosurgeon named Dr. Klein. After he did a number of tests, he announced that the surgery must be done right away. He also gave me a glimmer of hope when he said that everyone recovers at a different rate. Surely I couldn't be ready for my match only 21 days after surgery, could I?

While in the hospital, I was carted around in a wheelchair. I didn't exactly look like an Olympic athlete in top form. Could someone stop this nightmare now, I wondered?

I awoke after surgery, not knowing where I was and what was going on. I looked across the room and my eyes began to focus. Sitting there was my mentor Gene Kiniski. Gene and his son Nick made me a part of their family soon after I had moved to the West Coast. It was no surprise to me that he was the first person to visit me after my surgery.

Gene was a unique person. He had a way about him that made you think you could take on the world. He used to tell me that we – the athletes – did not have the same limits as other people because we were not "average." For some inexplicable reason, I believed him. Within a few minutes of our visit, Gene convinced me that because we train harder than anybody else in the world, we also recover faster. That made perfect sense to me. After all, I was on some pretty strong post-op pain medication!

In any event, Gene asked me what I wanted to do first and I mentioned that my top priority was to go to the bathroom. I was concerned that maybe I should not be walking so soon after my spine surgery, but Gene once again reminded me that I was not average. He was so convincing and, at the age of 21, who was I to tell him he was wrong? Gene told me to get up and walk over to the bathroom on my own. Obviously, the nurses didn't know that I was now superhuman and that I could walk unaided right after back surgery, but Gene knew.

I slowly sat up and got off the bed but, as I got to my feet and was about to take my first step, I fell face-first right onto the floor. My reflexes were so slow that I didn't even have time to put my hands out to brace the fall. My nose exploded on impact and blood gushed out everywhere.

Gene hurried over to help me; the nurses heard the thump as well and ran into my room. In a panic, they asked what had happened. Gene told them that I was just going to the bathroom and did not have the strength to walk yet. The nurses started to clean me up and got me back in my bed. I was scolded and told in no uncertain terms that I should stop with my foolish behavior and call if I was even thinking of moving from the bed. After the nurses left my room, Gene, undeterred, said "Oh well, let's give that a try again tomorrow" and proceeded to walk out of the room.

It had clearly not been a great beginning, but Gene came back every day and we did a little more each time. I started feeling stronger and more confident. It was hard not to with his recurring message that I was not average and that I would heal faster than anyone else.

I watched the opening ceremonies of the 1984 Olympics from my hospital bed. To say I was depressed would be an understatement. I saw my teammates walk into the stadium without me. This was what I had been working toward. This was my dream. A dream I had yet to fulfill.

I spent the second post-surgery week at the university, trying to convince the coaches and doctors that I had recovered sufficiently to join the team. I spent hours practicing how to stand straight and appear strong before I went to talk to anyone, just to try to persuade them that I was feeling fine.

Persistence finally paid off. I was told I could fly to Los Angeles to join the team. The coaches would take a look at my performance in some wrestling drills when I got there.

The media learned about this and it was generating a fair amount of news. The story was that flying me to L.A. was a nice gesture, but it was highly unlikely I would compete. To me, this was nonsense: I was not going all the way down there just to be a spectator.

Of course, these "naysayers" didn't know Gene Kiniski had persuaded me that I was not average. I actually believed him. It did not matter that no one else believed that I could compete. Gene knew I could, and I knew I could. That was all that mattered to me at the time.

Three weeks after my back surgery, I had my first match on my way to winning a Silver Medal in front of a sold-out crowd at the Anaheim Convention Center. On that day, my nightmare turned into a dream come true!

Too often we let naysayers convince us that something is impossible. With the help of my mentor, I learned firsthand that the popular saying "Where there's a will, there's a way" really is true.

We are products of our environment. The people we surround ourselves with either transfer us energy or take it away. Gene supplied me with enough energy to take on the world. Who do you have on your team that inspires you?

*A dream is your creative vision for your life in the future. You must break out of your current comfort zone and become comfortable with the unfamiliar and the unknown.*

-Denis Waitley

# Getting Uncomfortable

I remember, at age 21, returning from the 1984 Olympics with a silver medal in my hand and thinking that I would finally be able to relax.

Little did I know what was ahead of me! While en route home from the Olympics, someone recognized me on the plane and asked me to address the flight crew and passengers about my new Olympic experiences. Truth is; I didn't have a clue what to say. Being a good athlete doesn't necessarily make you a great communicator, so this request made me uncomfortable to say the least.

After arriving back in Vancouver, I discovered that much to my horror; I would now be expected to speak at sports banquets throughout British Columbia. I'll always remember my first post-Olympic speaking engagement – a huge gymnasium filled with students from three different schools. I was praying that someone else would talk for me and I could simply show people my medal, shake hands and smile a lot. We don't always get what we hope for.

After congratulating me on my achievement, the emcee handed the microphone over to me and asked me to address the crowd. As

## GET COMFORTABLE BEING UNCOMFORTABLE

I walked over to the podium, my heart began to race. Only a few weeks before that, I had been wrestling in front of 15,000 people – not to mention the millions that watched on TV – but that was wrestling. I was comfortable doing that; speaking in front of an audience, not so much.

I started talking and could feel beads of sweat building on my forehead. I hoped no one would notice this embarrassing bout of excessive persperation. I tried my best to will the sweat away, but it only got worse. It got so bad that a teacher actually walked up to me and handed me a towel! At that moment, I was ready to "throw in the towel."

I got through that first speech, drenched and embarrassed. I knew I needed to address my fear of speaking in public. Giving a presentation in front of an audience violated my self-imposed comfort zone – a sort of mental boundary I had put up to maintain a sense of security. I needed to confront my fear of public speaking and create an action plan. I understood that in moving out of my comfort zone, there would be challenges, but also celebrations, and new opportunities. I did not want fear to limit or restrict me – so I changed my mindset and took action!

I began to watch other people I respected speak to audiences. It was at that time that I learned the art of storytelling. People love to hear stories and I'd always loved telling them. It's something I incorporated into my speaking engagements from that point forward. It's helped me immeasurably in my career as a motivational speaker.

Though I felt like I was having a stroke at my first speaking engagement, that horrific experience taught me that being uncomfortable is actually a positive thing. It forces us to grow personally and professionally. Discomfort usually comes from trying out new experiences, so don't resist the unknown. When you are feeling uncomfortable, you're actually opening up a whole new world of opportunities for yourself. Take me for instance – that scared, sweaty, stumbling 21 year-old described earlier in the story is now a professional speaker! How many people in the audience that day predicted that would happen?!

What are you doing to make yourself uncomfortable?

*You gain strength, courage, and confidence by every experience
in which you really stop to look fear in the face.
You are able to say to yourself, 'I lived through this horror.
I can take the next thing that comes along.'*

-Eleanor Roosevelt

# The Wrestler

Nearly 30 years ago now, I was at a National Wrestling Championships. I had just won my first four wrestling matches and had the day off to wait for the finals to get underway.

It was bright and early in the morning when I arrived with the rest of the team at the sports complex. A sports reporter from the local newspaper asked me if I had time for an interview. I've never met a microphone I didn't like, even though everyone claims I talk so loud I don't need one! The reporter and I climbed into the stands a few rows up so we could sit and chat in relative silence.

We had just started the interview when the reporter noticed that a large group of his colleagues had gathered across the gym floor from us. Something was clearly up. The reporter apologized as he got up and asked if we could continue our interview later on. I said no problem. I was curious to find out what was going on, so I followed the reporter down the stands and across the gymnasium floor to a conference room below the gym. I opened the door and saw that the room was packed with media.

I had no idea why everyone was gathered together there, but I

## GET COMFORTABLE BEING UNCOMFORTABLE

knew something was happening. A wrestling team was huddled in the corner and one team member was crying.

The head coach walked up to the microphone and thanked the media and fans for coming out so early. He then announced that there had just been a terrible plane crash, and that no one had survived. The parents of one of the wrestlers had been flying down in a Cessna to watch their boy compete at Nationals when the father lost control of his plane and it went down. The room went silent. The coach then announced that, in light of this tragedy, he was pulling the team out of the tournament.

Then something truly remarkable happened. The wrestler whose parents were killed started to walk across the room towards the microphone. He was really trying hard to hold himself together as he prepared to address the crowd. He took a deep breath, fought back another round of tears and told everyone that he was staying in the tournament because that's what his parents would have wanted him to do. His dad used to train with him and never missed any of his meets. He knew how much his son loved to wrestle and would have been devastated if he withdrew from Nationals.

After the wrestler's brave address, an aggressive sports reporter pushed a microphone closer to the young man's mouth and, insensitively, reminded him that his parents wouldn't be there to watch him compete.

The wrestler hesitated for a second and replied with a line I will never forget:

"Yes, my parents will be watching. They'll just be in a stand a little higher up today."

## BOB MOLLE

The room went silent and I officially became a big fan of this guy.

After the emotional press conference, I walked up to the main lobby where the draw was held, so I could see how the wrestler had done so far in the tournament. He had lost his first match, so the best he could do was finish third. I, like everyone in the stands, watched every one of his matches with bated breath. The whole arena was rooting for him.

The word *courage* is often overused. Is it really that courageous to ask someone out on a date, to put a friend in their place, or ask your boss for a raise? These actions require you to take action and show assertiveness – two fantastic qualities – but I wouldn't go as far as saying they are acts of courage. When you're lucky enough to witness *true* courage, it leaves its mark. It changes the way you look at adversity in your own life, and provides proof of just how strong the human spirit really is.

The wrestler won his next three matches, all in sudden-death overtime. He did indeed finish third at Nationals and you couldn't help but think he was right about there being someone "up there" cheering him on.

Since that day, I've thought of this courageous wrestler every time I've faced intense pressure or adversity. I could not imagine how much pain this young man had after he heard of his parent's sudden and shocking passing. During the most difficult time of his life, he found it within himself to create something positive by energizing and inspiring thousands. That is true courage.

No matter what life throws at you, will you find the courage to do what needs to be done?

*And let me tell you, you boys of America, that there is no higher inspiration to any man to be a good man, a good citizen, and a good son, brother, or father, than the knowledge that you come from honest blood.*

-John Sergeant Wise

# Everyday Superstar

I've known Dave for quite a while. He comes into the YMCA nearly every day. About a year ago, Dave was absent from the Y for an entire week. It wasn't like him at all, and I began to become concerned about whether something might have happened to him. But sure enough, Dave returned to working out at the gym the following week.

Dave is one of those rare people that ALWAYS has a smile on his face and a kind word to say. His positive attitude is infectious and you can tell it comes naturally to him. It's not an act, it's just who he is. Sometimes he asks me to time him while he does sprints around the track. He is certainly never short on energy.

When I saw him again after his absence I called out to him from across the gym. Dave walked over and greeted me with a handshake. I told him I missed him and asked where he had been. He answered that he had been in Victoria, B.C. What was he doing out there? He was running the half marathon and he had a fantastic result. Running a half-marathon is a tremendous feat, but let's face it, we all know someone who's done it. Running is becoming an increasingly popular leisure activity and if you train long enough while avoiding injury, a 13.1 mile run is well within most people's reach. What's so special about the fact that Dave finished this run? Well, I forgot to mention that Dave is 84 years old!

One day at the Y, Dave kneeled down beside me while I was doing some sit-ups. It was pretty unusual to see Dave remain still in any position for long, so I wondered what was up. He asked me if I made a habit of reading the newspaper. Slightly confused by the question, I confirmed that I did, and asked why.

Dave then told me that he had just lost his wife of 60 years, Norma. I stopped doing sit-ups and sat up in stunned silence for a few seconds before doing my best to let him know how sorry I was to hear of Norma's passing.

After the workout, I went home to look through the obituaries. Norma's funeral was to be held the following day. I showed up at the funeral and sat in the back. During the ceremony, Dave spoke with so much pride and affection about his wife, whom he met when she was only 10 years old, as well as his four children, eight grandchildren, and four great-grandchildren.

At the end of the ceremony, he walked right up to me and gave me a long hug. Then he looked up and told me he was glad I came. He actually told everyone at the funeral that "the big guy at the back of the room" was his bodyguard!

For as long as I've known him, Dave has always been grateful for everything he had. I really wanted to know how he managed to stay so positive. After all, a person who has lived 84 years on this earth surely has had his share of heartache and disappointment.

However, Dave's attitude surprised me. His "secret" to a happy life is very simple: to him, every day he is healthy and able to spend with his kids, grandkids and great-grandkids is a gift to be treasured and enjoyed. And enjoy life he does. Since he is in such great shape, he can still throw a football or a Frisbee, shoot a puck, and play baseball. Dave knows exactly what keeps him motivated. He had found his "why."

It's no wonder that I find myself inspired by Dave. He continually teaches me to appreciate the most important things in life: family, friends, health and happiness.

Wayne Dyer, an internationally renowned self-development expert, explains that motivation is when you get hold of an idea and don't let go of it until you make it a reality. Inspiration is the reverse—when an idea gets hold of you and you feel compelled to let that impulse or energy carry you along. You get to a point where you realize that you're no longer in charge, that there's a driving force inside you that can't be stopped.

Do you know who (or what) inspires you? Have you found your "why"? It's never too late. If you don't have a source of inspiration yet, isn't it time to find one?

*Before success comes in any man's life, he's sure to meet with much temporary defeat and, perhaps some failures. When defeat overtakes a man, the easiest and the most logical thing to do is to quit. That's exactly what the majority of men do.*

-Napoleon Hill

# Resisting the Easy Way Out

I heard a piercing scream and my heart started pounding. I ran over to my youngest son, Sean, and found him rolling on the ground, clutching his knee in agony. I literally felt sick to my stomach.

Sean was just finishing his 12th grade of high school. All in all, it had been a good year for him: he had just finished his football season, his team had won the provincial championships, and he also had a good shot at winning the provincials in wrestling. A number of universities had offered him scholarships. It seemed like all he had to do was keep on training hard and a world of opportunities would open up for him.

However, life sometimes throws us a curveball.

After a few examinations of Sean's injury, it was obvious that his knee was torn up quite badly and surgery was the only option. All of a sudden, Sean's goals and dreams appeared to be dashed.

From a "can't miss" prospect, Sean had morphed into the category of "damaged goods." University coaches and all the other people who were excited about him before the injury stopped calling. Sean's life was put on hold. He was in limbo.

## GET COMFORTABLE BEING UNCOMFORTABLE

We knew that delaying the surgery was not the answer. Sean would have to get back in the gym as soon as possible so he could maintain his upper body strength. We found a good surgeon and he informed us that the operation on Sean's knee would last about an hour.

Three hours later and there was still no sign of Sean or the surgeon. When you are waiting for news about the well-being of your son or daughter, three hours feels like an eternity. Finally, the doctor came out of the operating room, said the surgery went well, but he had to use a couple of pieces from a cadaver to put Sean's knee back together. He told us the prognosis was good but warned us that Sean was going to be in a lot of pain – in other words, his recovery would be an uphill road.

At times like these, it's easy to feel like you're the only one going through such hardship. As clichéd as it sounds, it really is important to remember that someone always has it worse than you do. You don't have to spend much time in a hospital to find an example of this.

As we waited, a promising young downhill skier was brought into the next room. We later found out that she had to have three ligaments reconstructed in her knee. For anyone that knows anything about knee injuries, making a full recovery from even one ligament reconstruction is difficult enough. Who knows if this poor girl will ever get to ski again? If Sean works hard enough, he'll certainly be able to return to playing football and wrestling. Seeing that girl gave him an appreciation of that fact.

The lesson to learn from my son's experience is that even seemingly perfect plans can go sideways sometimes. Life doesn't always deliver a perfect road map. There's always going to be unexpected speed bumps on our path. Some of those bumps may feel as insurmountable as the highest mountain.

During this long recovery, my wife and I are doing all we can to keep Sean's spirits up. We want to keep him focused on the positive events in his future rather than the unfortunate predicament he had found himself in.

Sean hasn't fully recovered from his injury yet, but he is doing progressively better and the universities are showing interest in him again. He has a goal now, something tangible to look forward to, and his busted knee will not stop him from realizing his dreams.

We can get through tough times, and even learn something positive from the experience, if we are persistent and focused on our ultimate dream or goal. Remember: the bump on the road is not the end of the road.

Have you ever given up on a dream because you hit a speed bump? How do you feel about it? Does it leave you thinking about what could have been? We cannot change the past, but from this day forward, remember that speed bumps are as much a part of your journey as the open stretches of highway. The things we most appreciate in life are the things we've had to work the hardest for. What are you willing to commit to that you can appreciate the rest of your life?

*Insanity: doing the same thing over and over again and expecting different results.*

-Albert Einstein

# The Shake Up

When my children were young, my wife Karen and I loved the time leading up to Christmas: the tree decorating, the stockings, the presents, the anticipation, and the notes our children left for Santa. In a child's life, there is nothing more magical than the idea of a man in a red suit arriving in the middle of the night with all the gifts he or she had truly wished for all year long. For parents, it's a wonderful time as well – not only seeing their children's excited anticipation, but also their good behavior, since Santa's gift-giving is contingent on being nice, not naughty.

But as my children got older and learned the truth about Santa, the excitement was gone from the celebration that had once captivated their imagination. Christmas had become a frenzy of mundane gift-giving – upgrading to the newest video game or filling up a closet with clothes they didn't need. The magic was gone; in fact, the kids could not remember the Christmases past with any clarity – one holiday celebration blended into the next. It was time for a change!

Karen and I wanted to show our children that appreciating and enjoying life was not dependent upon having the latest gadget or the

## GET COMFORTABLE BEING UNCOMFORTABLE

coolest pair of designer jeans. We wanted to offer them a much more valuable gift – an adventure and memories that would last a lifetime. A chance to expand their horizons and open their minds.

So we asked them what they thought about a month-long family trip. We could immediately see the excitement on their faces. We talked about the Seven Wonders of the World and the children began to focus on visiting the Great Wall of China. They learned that the Wall could be seen all the way from the Moon. That's powerful and inspiring stuff, so the energy and anticipation were gaining momentum daily.

The trip turned out to be not only exciting and fascinating, but also a life-altering experience for the whole family. The fun started when we landed in Beijing and got conned into a "taxi ride" to the hotel.

Mistake number one, which we discovered only the next day, when we had an informal briefing from some airline attendants we met at breakfast. They recommended we only hire taxis through the hotel from that point forward. Apparently Beijing is full of unregistered taxi drivers. Yikes!

The next day, we got picked up by our new, and much more legitimate taxi driver, Charlie. He was not only our driver, but an interpreter and tour guide as well. When he picked us up, he asked me what I wanted to do and where I wanted to go. He quickly figured out that I was not the decision maker in the family.

Charlie asked the children a question, but because of his heavy accent, they were not sure what he was saying. Finally, my eldest son Ryan figured out that he was asking who the boss in the family was. The kids responded emphatically that it was "Mom!"

At the next light, Charlie turned to us and said, pointing first to Karen and then to me: "You Tiger and him Little Potato!"

The entire family burst out laughing. Charlie found something that was uncommon in his culture, a female boss, which made this ride educational not only for us but also for him. All the kids replied at the same time: "Yes, Dad is the Little Potato and Mom is the Tiger." Charlie was happy to know who would answer his questions from now on. Not surprisingly, these two labels continue to be used around our house to this day.

Our plan was to visit Tiananmen Square to see where the world watched, in 1989, a young Chinese man's standoff against a tank, but en route we had a strange experience. The people in the vehicles that we passed by were clearly staring at us. Some people even waved.

My family obviously isn't Chinese, but apart from that, what was so bizarre about us? Charlie stopped at a red light and a bus pulled beside us. All the passengers ran over to one side of the bus to take a look in our van. We were feeling like animals in a zoo exhibit.

Ryan finally asked Charlie what was going on.

"Have these people never seen tourists before?"

Charlie pointed to our heads and we didn't understand him at first. Then we realized that it was our hair. Karen's is curly blonde, and our three children have almost white-blonde hair. Charlie said the Chinese found us "beautiful," although we believe he actually meant to say we were seen as "freaks." You certainly don't get to feel unique and special just for having blonde hair in Canada, so the kids we're really eating it up. They got to feel what it's like to be in the spotlight, and I think they loved it.

## GET COMFORTABLE BEING UNCOMFORTABLE

Next, Charlie dropped us off by the Forbidden City and we arranged a pickup point. We assumed that since this was a major tourist attraction, no one would pay particular attention to us – or our hair. But we continued to draw crowds of spectators. People approached us with cameras. We thought they wanted us to take a picture of them but what they really wanted was to pose in a picture with us.

My youngest son Sean was the most requested participant. He was eleven at the time and his hair was even more white-blonde than his older siblings. One of the people who wanted his picture spoke some English. We asked why they wanted a photograph of a complete stranger. She explained that Sean was fascinating to them because he was a "baby-man." Apparently, he had the face of a baby but was as tall as a man!

Growing up in Canada, our children were used to an array of ethnicities. Differences are expected and are the norm. That first day of our trip, however, the children learned that the "melting pot" concept is not as common everywhere else. It was clear that many of the people we encountered had never seen anyone up-close and in person who looked like us.

Later that day, we made it to the Great Wall. It was truly awesome. It went on forever! We played a bit of catch with the football that we had brought along. We hung out for about an hour in one of the forts and talked about what it might have been like to be a soldier back in the day, watching for intruders coming up the mountain.

No book or history lesson could replace what my children saw, heard and felt that day. No video game or article of clothing could "wow" them like this one experience.

When we're going with the flow, it's easy to fall into a rut. You get so comfortable that your life is on auto-pilot. After a while, life becomes so monotonous that you can't distinguish one day from the next. This is no way to live and ensures that you'll never achieve any of your goals. If what you've been doing doesn't excite you, it's time to shake things up. What do you need to do to bring a sense of awe and adventure back into your life?

*If you're an underdog, mentally disabled, physically disabled, if you don't fit in, if you're not as pretty as the others, you can still be a hero.*

-Steve Guttenberg

# How David Beat Goliath

The other day, I started thinking about times when I've felt an opponent was completely undefeatable. I thought of 1988, when I played with the Winnipeg Blue Bombers. The media and the fans were calling it a "rebuilding year." A lot of great football players had retired the year before, and we knew we simply weren't as experienced or as strong as some of the other teams in the league.

On a personal level, the season did not start well. During the last game of the pre-season against the Ottawa Rough Riders, I was blocking the guy in front of me when I felt someone tumble across my knee. I heard a popping sound and fell in a lot of pain. I rolled on the turf hoping that the pain would subside. When I looked up, the trainers were yelling at me to "relax."

How the heck do you relax when you can barely breathe?! They finally got me to lie back on the turf so they could get a better look at my knee. After I was tricked into "relaxing," (which is really an impossibility, all things considered), the trainer tugged at my knee as it was slowly moved one way and then the other. I could tell by the look on the trainer's face (and the level of my pain) that all was not well. My teammates picked me up and carried me to the sidelines. I would need surgery and my season was over.

As expected, it had been a difficult season. We lost our final three games, but somehow managed to squeak into the playoffs. Unfortunately, we were up against the Toronto Argonauts, who were by far the most heavily favored team in 1988.

The Argos had a 14-4 record and they viewed us Bombers as nothing more than a little speed bump on their road to victory – or so they thought. Our team had heard a rumor that the Argos had already purchased their tickets to the Grey Cup before they even played us! We were obviously angry about that. No one was giving us any chance of winning, especially since we were going to be playing on the road in Toronto.

According to Malcolm Gladwell's article, *How David Beats Goliath,* an underdog can beat a favourite 63.6 percent of the time. How is this possible? Gladwell argues it's feasible if an "unconventional strategy" is employed. The Bombers coach that year was Mike Riley. He was an exceptional person: kind, thoughtful and well prepared. If it benefited him, Coach Riley had no qualms about employing unconventional strategies…and that's exactly what he did against the Argos.

In our game against Toronto, Coach Riley inserted a big, strapping 265-lbs. lineman to replace a smaller linebacker. No one had ever seen this before. The Toronto coaches had no idea how to handle this and under Coach Riley's guidance, we executed his plan as though we had been practicing it all season long.

The extra lineman that was put into play ran over the Argos' running backs numerous times to sack the quarterback. Toronto simply couldn't contain the big man and was helpless against a team that had done something totally unconventional to win.

For the record, the Blue Bombers won the game 27-11.

I suggest that next time you are up against a superior opponent – or one that is believed to be stronger and better –start by assessing your own weaknesses and then figure out a strategy that minimizes them. In other words, focus on the solution rather than the problem. Remember: when you utilize a strategy that no one is expecting, the odds are in your favor 63.6 percent of the time. That is how David can beat Goliath. What unconventional strategy are you applying in your life?

Bob defeats Egypt's Hassan El-Haded in the semi-finals at the 1984 Olympics in Los Angeles

Bob in action with the Winnipeg Blue Bombers

Bob with Steve Rodehutskors shortly after their 1988 Grey Cup victory

Bob poses with his Olympic medal and the Grey Cup

Bob pulling double duties: coaching and "Daddy Daycare"

Bob embracing his mentor, Gene Kiniski

Bob coaching kids football in Winnipeg

The Molle's in China, 2004

Bob participating in Ironman Canada in Penticton, B.C.

The "Molle Crue": (from left to right) Sean, Karen, Ryan, Bob, Sarah

*The greatest wealth is to live content with little.*

-Plato

# True Wealth

A couple of years ago, the Molle family took a month-long trip to the South Pacific, making stops in the Cook Islands; New Zealand; Australia; and on the way back, Fiji. We were confident that the trip would be fun-filled, safe and interesting. There was only one stop we were somewhat concerned about – Fiji.

We had heard some very mixed reviews about the island, especially when it came to its political stability. There was apparently great tension between the indigenous Fijian and Indo-Fijian communities. The tension even caused a few coup d'états and a constitutional crisis in the recent past. We had even discussed cancelling the Fiji visit and staying in Australia for an extra week.

We learned that the political uprisings were centered in the urban areas and that rural Fiji was less likely to be affected, so we opted to stay out of the cities. When we travel, we often do so with very little planning in advance. We simply make reservations when we arrive and kind of leave things up in the air. Travelling without a plan is way more fun. Trust me.

For the Fiji trip though, we figured it would be smart to book our

## GET COMFORTABLE BEING UNCOMFORTABLE

entire five-night stay in advance, so we booked through the internet at a "Backpackers Resort," an oxymoron if there ever was one. We had booked a safari tent in the jungle, a stone's throw to the beach. It was paradise. We have seen beautiful beaches before and this beach rivaled any of them. But what was truly remarkable about this beach was not the sand; it was the temperature of the water. First thing in the morning, you could climb out of your tent and go for a swim and feel like you just stepped into the bathtub. It was glorious!

We were pleasantly surprised to meet the other travelers at the "resort;" young couples from all over the world. Many of them were professionals who were travelling on a budget. They were fun, interesting people who lacked the "five star attitude" you often encounter on a tropical holiday.

It wasn't so much the fellow tourists that made this trip memorable though, it was the Fijian people. It has to be one of the friendliest places on the planet. When everyone you pass says "Hello" with a smile, it's my kind of place! The Fijians are a special group of people; proud, happy, and deeply interested in those who come to visit. We've often been treated to first-class service, but you always get the feeling you're just another tourist. The Fijians are so genuine that they make you feel special. While this was not a large complex, within hours of our arrival the staff knew all of our names, where we were from, what "hut" we were in, and what we liked to drink.

I'm an early riser. I mean really early. It's not uncommon for me to be out of bed by as early as 4 or 5 in the morning. It drives my wife crazy! And changing time zones certainly doesn't help. In Fiji, I was awake just as the sun was rising. Usually vacationers are just stumbling home when I'm starting my day, but there was none of that at this backpackers resort. Nothing was open at 5 a.m. and there was no one to talk to, so I simply wandered around the area taking in whatever I could find to look at.

I began to sense I was being followed. I looked behind me and noticed that a security guard was following me; analyzing my every move. After this went on for nearly an hour, the security guard finally approached me and asked if I was lost. I later found out that I was being followed because security figured I was a lost drunk or a very heavy-footed thief!

The security guard's name was John. He was a stocky, muscular man in his late 30s. He had a shaved head just like mine, so we immediately hit it off. He was friendly and really easy to talk to. John and I began to share stories about our lives and our families. He worked every night at the resort and only made about $10 per day. He'd been in the military for a number of years, and had deployed overseas to do peacekeeping work. He did it primarily for the money, and thanks to his time in the military, he'd been able to build a house with a cement floor. Most of the locals don't have such luxuries. John was contemplating doing another tour so he could further develop his house.

In the following days, I got to know John quite well. He was a big fan of sports, and wanted to know what sports I had been involved with in my younger days. I told him that I'd played professional football, which he simply called "gridiron." Then I told him a bit about being an Olympic wrestler. As soon as the word 'wrestler' left my lips, John was beside himself with excitement.

## GET COMFORTABLE BEING UNCOMFORTABLE

"Wrestler! You we're a wrestler?!"

Finally, some proper recognition! I've been telling people for years about my wrestling and no one had ever been as excited about it as John. I began to like the guy even more.

John would follow me down to the beach each morning and watch me do all my exercises. He was a workout buff too and we exchanged exercise ideas back and forth. One morning, John walked up to me and asked if my family wanted to join his family for dinner. I readily agreed. Some of the other travellers at the resort were shocked that I was bringing my family to the village. They warned me about the potential dangers, but I paid no attention to them. I had total confidence that John was a genuine guy.

The next night, my family and I took a cab to the village. I had asked John that morning if there was anything I could bring. He mentioned that I should bring some "kava." We had learned that the roots of the kava plant are used to produce a drink with sedative and anaesthetic properties. It wasn't available at the resort, but was easy to find in the village.

Twenty minutes down the road and through a number of beat-up dirt roads we arrived at the village. It was very much third-world and there were no windows or doors on the houses. I walked up to greet John when we arrived at his place. His whole extended family was waiting to welcome my family. John's family and neighbours shared a dug out hole in the ground that was filled with rocks. They had been heating the rocks all day with a fire over top of them. In Fiji, this is what they call a barbecue.

John's neighbour had some pork that he wanted to share with

everyone. John's nephews were down at the ocean looking to spear some fish for this special feast. We were also going to have some local root vegetables and another dish wrapped in leaves and cooked on the "barbecue." While the women cooked, we were invited to sit on the floor and join in the kava ceremony. There was a ritualistic chant that went along with the process.

I looked outside and noticed that more and more people were approaching John's house. Lots of children were peeking inside and staring at me. A little unsettled, I asked John why everyone was staring into his house.

"To see you of course. It's not every day that a wrestler from the WWF comes to our village. They wanted to see if they recognized you from TV."

I guess Fijians didn't know anything about Olympic-style wrestling, they only knew of the fake stuff they saw on TV. Karen overheard the conversation and tried to explain the difference between Olympic wrestling and the theatrical pro wrestling. John was very confused.

"Just let it go Karen," I said.

Word spread like wildfire about the WWF Superstar having dinner in that tiny Fijian village. There were even rumours that Hulk Hogan was in town! More and more village people started coming by John's house to get a good look at me.

John's mother got everyone sitting on the floor for the kava ceremony. One gentleman sat and squeezed water through a nylon sock where the crushed Kava root had been placed. It looked like dirt water after he was done with it, but I was up for the adventure. This was not a quick drink. We had to repeat the ritual before anyone could drink, and the custom was to drink one person at a time.

After about five rounds of drinking kava, John informed me that the chief of the village was coming over to meet us. The village chief advised us that we were now honorary members of their village. The next time we came to Fiji, we did not have to stay at any resort; we could simply stay with them.

Over dinner, we discussed the tough economic times plaguing the world. The men simply shrugged their shoulders and noted that they didn't let the economy affect their lives. All they needed to buy was sugar and flour. They could grow or raise everything else, or find it in the ocean. It was refreshing to see how happy people could be with very little material wealth. For them, having a happy family and a sense of community was far more important. The kids in the village seemed very happy, even without things like video games and TV. They played rugby, fished, swam and enjoyed the outdoors. Everyone likes to consider places like Fiji "poor." I do not agree. My adopted Fijian village has more wealth than we could ever dream of having.

No matter what anyone tells you, it's the simple things that make you happiest: family, friends, health and sense of community. Nurture these things and you will lead a happier life. Are you smart enough to be simple?

*Nothing brings me more happiness than trying to help the most vulnerable people in society. It is a goal and an essential part of my life - a kind of destiny. Whoever is in distress can call on me. I will come running wherever they are.*

-Princess Diana

# Are There Angels on Earth?

It was 1984 and I was getting ready to attend the Canadian Olympic Wrestling Team training camp. The only problem was that no one knew where it was going to be held. Wrestling teams from east and west were jockeying to host the National Training Camp. To end the dispute, someone decided that Regina would host the event – right in the heart of Canada! Since I grew up in Saskatoon, I was happy to head back home to Saskatchewan, though others may not have shared this sentiment.

While getting ready for the Los Angeles Olympics, the team would be living at the University of Regina dormitory. I was not keen on living in a dorm, so I called up my Aunt Dickie who lives close by to see if she would take me in for the duration of the camp. She agreed without hesitation.

Since that time I have dropped in on Dickie to spend the night on various occasions while driving across the country. In fact, my wife and children have all crashed at Dickie's at one time or another, and usually with no, or very little, notice. But that did not matter to Dickie; we always felt welcomed, and were fed and cared for as if she had been expecting us for weeks. That is just the kind of lady Dickie is.

For five years, Dickie followed the Western Hockey League schedule closely so she could cheer on my son Ryan when his team was in town to play the Pats. She would watch the game and shout out encouragement for her nephew, but, most importantly, she would have to be ready to give him his rhubarb pie at the end of the game - along with a hug of course!

Dickie's thoughtfulness knows no bounds. For example, she always sends out cards to people who are sick, injured, graduating or getting married; whatever the occasion – happy or sad – Dickie lets us know that she is thinking of us.

You may think that there is nothing extraordinary about someone who treats her family in this manner. But that is the remarkable thing about my Aunt Dickie, she treats everyone with the same love and attention. If there is an angel on this earth, it is Dickie.

She grew up in a family of thirteen children in Englefeld, Saskatchewan. She is now 81 years old. Dickie and my mother were both nurses. Nurses seem to have an endless supply of empathy and compassion, but Dickie's generosity is truly exceptional.

A few years ago, she was out on her daily walk when she was hit by a truck while crossing the road. The truck had been turning left and did not see her. Dickie went flying through the air and landed on the pavement stunned and quite sore. The young truck driver immediately ran over to apologize. Dickie told him not worry because she was "just fine."

The driver felt bad about hitting her, but Dickie kept on consoling *him.* She learned that he had a wife and daughter who would be turning two the following week. They had exchanged contact information and Dickie reassured the young man that she was not hurt, even though she was in quite a bit of pain. That next week Dickie bought his daughter a birthday present and dropped it by his house. She wanted to make sure he was feeling better. "I knew he would be feeling bad so I wanted to let him know that everything was okay," she said.

Since retiring from nursing, Dickie dedicates her time to those who are in need. She counsels young pregnant women who have no place to turn. She works at a centre that feeds and provides clothing for men who are trying to get off the streets. She does caregiver respite work taking care of sick and dying patients, so their loved ones can get a short break from their 24-hour, seven-day-a week responsibility. With these commitments, you would think that Dickie does not have a spare minute in her day, but she still manages to squeeze in time to assist paralyzed patients who are recovering in the hospital. Dickie told me that many of them are suicidal after their accidents so they need help and love. She said that it is important that she does this, so that these people can "reach their full potential."

Helping to care for the sick or injured may be expected from a former nurse, but what I find remarkable is that Dickie also volunteers at a program dealing with sexual offenders who are now out of prison trying to start their lives over again. She goes to church with them; sometimes her church, sometimes theirs. She visits, has coffee, and listens to them. She makes sure they know how much she cares. Dickie knows what these men have done; they have committed horrible, violent sexual assaults. They have ruined the lives of innocent women. How can she do this work? She says that if she does not help them and love them, who will? Her job is not to judge but, rather, to provide them with unconditional love.

Dickie gets her strength and conviction from her faith; she tells me that "God will never give us more than we can handle." At 81, Dickie proves time and time again how much we can handle. I asked Dickie how she became such a caring person who dedicates her existence to helping others? She proudly talks about her 40-year-marriage to Ed, the love of her life. She says he taught her how to live her life and that every day with him was a gift. Unfortunately, Ed passed away from cancer in 1994.

Dickie's life was shattered, her grief and pain overwhelming. A year after Ed's passing, the pain had not begun to subside and Dickie knew she had to take action to shake off the despair. She decided to pack up her car and drive to the West Coast. The idea terrified her; she had never lived alone and certainly had never taken a trip like this by herself. She says that it was like a suicide trip that would either make her or break her. She stopped at various places along the way: Medicine Hat, Calgary, Invermere, Chase, Horseshoe Bay, Port Alberni, Victoria, Vancouver and Kelowna. What did Dickie find? As she puts it: "There was love all the way." No matter where she went, there were people she loved and who loved her back. She found out she could live alone, but that she would never be truly alone.

Dickie says that she is "blessed," because of all the people in her life who love her. When she turned 80, she had a full week of parties to attend because so many people wanted to celebrate with her. There is truly never a dull moment in her life. We have all heard the phrase "what you give out, you get back." Dickie's life is an example of how accurate that statement is.

There are so many lonely, bored and unhappy people in this world looking for relief in a bottle, a pill, or at the mall. Dickie has learned that giving herself, her love, and her time is the secret to happiness. Has Dickie discovered the secret formula to a happy life? Can we all learn from her?

*Happiness is when what you think, what you say, and what you do are in harmony.*

-Mohandas Gandhi

# Creating Harmony

It was the early morning in Halifax, Nova Scotia and I was just about to board a flight to Calgary, connecting through Toronto. I'd taken hundreds of flights over my years as an athlete and Sales Manager. I don't even remember most of them. This journey stuck with me though, and I won't soon forget the lesson it provided on human interaction.

Since I am 6'4," airplane seats are uncomfortable at the best of times. Flying across a country as large as Canada creates challenges for me. Just as we were about to land in Toronto, the flight attendant advised that anyone who was connecting to Calgary would be delayed. A few moans could be heard throughout the airplane. A couple of minutes later, there was another announcement indicating that the connecting flight to Calgary was now cancelled. After muttering under my breath for a moment, I went to the gate for more information. The next flight was over five hours away. It was also in another terminal so I had to pick up my bags and take a shuttle over there. Pearson International is a massive airport.

I found my bags, located the bus, loaded my bags and took a seat at the back. As soon as I sat down, I leaned my head against the window and fell asleep. Moments later, I awoke to the sound of another passenger berating the driver because we had not yet moved. More people began yelling at the bus driver and before long the bus driver was reacting.

I awoke in a daze and had no idea why all these people were arguing with the bus driver. I slid over in my seat, looked around and saw an elderly couple standing outside the bus. Their bags and boxes were all lined up in front of the bus door. There were ten pieces of luggage sitting at the curb side to be exact. I tried to calm one of the disgruntled passengers on my way to asking the bus driver if the couple outside the bus was the reason for the delay.

The bus driver was quite agitated. He explained to me that it was not his job to load all this baggage onto the bus. In an attempt to calm the situation, I joked that I hadn't gotten my exercise that day and told him I would be glad to load the bags. As I looked back at all the angry passengers on that packed bus, it amazed me that no one else was willing to help. Every one of them was disturbed that the bus wasn't moving, but no one was doing anything about it.

Maybe this was an example of the "bystander problem" I read about in Malcolm Gladwell's the *Tipping Point.* A couple scientists from Columbia University and New York University realized that the single greatest factor in predicting helping behaviour was the number of witnesses to the event. They found that when only one witness is present, they will rush to someone's aid approximately 85 percent of the time. When you increase the number of witnesses to four, the probability of someone helping is only 31%. There must have been

## GET COMFORTABLE BEING UNCOMFORTABLE

at least 50 people on this bus. Maybe the feeling of responsibility had become too diffused. Either that or everyone else on the bus lacked compassion.

I walked up to the elderly couple and asked if I could help them and I soon realized that they didn't speak English. They were quite old, petite and the lady walked with a cane. I decided to get her on the bus first. As soon as I got her up the stairs I remembered that there were only a few seats left at the very back. I asked a man in the front row if he would mind moving so I could keep this elderly woman close to the front. He seemed slightly offended by my request but eventually moved. The woman beside him caught on and moved so that the husband could sit beside his wife. Finally, some cooperation! I walked back outside and brought her husband on board and then loaded all their bags and their boxes. After each load, I was expecting someone to come give me a hand. It seemed everyone was too "busy" to help. All of these irate travellers just sat and waited for me to finish putting the luggage on the bus by myself.

After finishing with the luggage, I checked the couples' boarding passes to figure out which gate they needed to be at. It wasn't the same gate as mine, but I would go to theirs anyway. I had five hours until my flight. What did it matter what gate I went to?

We arrived at their gate and I helped them off the bus. Through motions and gestures, I indicated I would help them to their gate. I asked the bus driver to hold back a few seconds while I found a couple of trolleys. I filled the trolleys and wheeled them to the gate. After I finished unloading all the luggage and boxes, I looked over at the elderly lady with the cane. She had a tear in her eye and had opened up her arms for a hug. She was only about 5 feet tall, so I had to test the old knees in crouching down to hug her. Her husband also gave me a big hug, thanked me for my help, and we said goodbye.

When it comes to reaching our potential, Eastern philosophy teaches us that we have an obligation to create *harmony* whenever possible. Next time you witness a conflict, or see someone who needs help, will you be the one to create harmony?

*Football is like life - it requires perseverance, self-denial, hard work, sacrifice, dedication and respect for authority.*

-Vince Lombardi

# Smitty

I have had the privilege of coaching football for over 15 years and have worked with 6-year-olds all the way to 17 and 18-year old high school students. No matter what the age group, it is fascinating to watch tryouts. These youngsters come from all walks of life; some are there because their parents signed them up, some because they want the cool jacket, and others just like the idea of hitting someone. A few join because their best friend did and some do it for the right reason: they love the game of football. But Smitty was different from all the others.

He grew up in the U.K. and had only seen football on TV. To him, football was what we in North America call soccer. The pre-season always starts with equipment pick up. Typically the boys go from one station to another and pick up what they need. The coaches help with sizing and answer any questions the kids may have. Smitty had absolutely no idea what gear he needed. He was completely baffled by the equipment we had handed him; in fact, he had no idea how to put it on.

## GET COMFORTABLE BEING UNCOMFORTABLE

He corralled me in the corner of the gymnasium where he could discuss in private how the various pieces of padding fit together. As I worked with him through the equipment process, I began to consider the challenges that Smitty was facing. He was extremely shy and – as if his shyness wasn't enough – he also had a speech impediment. It was a struggle for him to talk. Now he was trying to learn a new game, at a new school, and in a different country. I sensed the intense discomfort he was feeling and thought that being on this team was going to be tough for him.

During the drills, Smitty's confusion became obvious, but because of his speech problems he seldom spoke. He usually waited until the end of practice to talk to me. Clearly, he felt more comfortable talking to me because he knew I wouldn't make fun of the way he talked. I guess I understood why he always approached me; I was the one who had helped him through his equipment confusion. I think he trusted me because of that. I understood this and worked with him after practice.

Smitty consistently worked hard, but with absolutely no previous football experience, he was facing a steep learning curve. To complicate things, his mother was not happy that he was on the team. She thought it would affect his schoolwork. But Smitty stayed on the team and came to practice every day without fail.

Smitty eventually began to understand his position and was developing the skills he needed to play it. As we progressed through the season, he continued to improve. From our after-practice discussions, I could tell that not only was he mastering the game, he had also learned to love it! He wanted to excel.

## BOB MOLLE

When he started, Smitty had no clue how to tackle. Any football coach worth his salt knows that in football "the low man always wins." Smitty stood up as tall as he could and tried to bear-hug the ball carrier. However, slowly but surely, Smitty learned to get low and make a tackle – he would become giddy with excitement when the tackling drills would begin. He was starting to learn the fundamentals of the game us North Americans call football and I began to notice a smirk on his face when the drills would start. There was no doubt about it - he loved this game.

Still, Smitty continued coming to me after every practice with his questions about the game and how he could get better. By mid-season, he had earned a starting position on the team. He learned the plays and his position. His fitness and strength had improved. His confidence had grown by leaps and bounds.

Something remarkable happened during our second playoff game. We were losing by 4 points with only minutes remaining. We needed to get the ball back and we were running out of time. If we lost, our season was over. Our coaching staff put our best poker faces on because we didn't want the kids to know that panic was setting in. Everyone had worked too hard for the season to end at that point. We had to get that ball back.

That's when Smitty beat his man wide, picked up speed and torpedoed himself helmet first into the opposing quarterback's gut. The impact popped the ball out of the quarterback's hand as he fell to the ground. As surprised as anyone, Smitty scooped it up as if he had done it a million times before and ran in to the end zone for the game-winning touchdown. It was textbook perfect. The entire team ran onto the field to congratulate him. At the end of the game, Smitty was carried off the field on the shoulders of his teammates! It was just like the scene in my one of my favourite football movies, *Rudy.*

It was a golden moment, but I never really appreciated how much team spirit can build self-esteem and confidence until our football banquet weeks later. I met Smitty's parents and told them how much I had enjoyed working with their son. Smitty's mother interrupted me and said,"Excuse me my love, you don't understand. Since Smitty joined the team, his marks have improved and, in fact, he now plans to attend university to become an engineer. I can't thank you enough for what this team has done for my son."

She reached for my hands, took me aside and said in her thick British accent, "When in my son's life is he ever going to be picked up and carried on people's shoulders again? This is only something a team can do! He now has 30 friends for life. For that experience, I can never thank you enough!"

Smitty's transformation from the beginning of the season to the end was nothing short of a miracle. Being part of the football team turned out to be the catalyst for building his self-esteem and it had given him an opportunity to succeed. It was hard for Smitty to find the nerve to approach me after each practice and speak to me about things he did not understand. But he found the courage to do it. He persevered through his speech difficulties and shyness not only to learn a new sport, but to excel at it as well. Even though Smitty's mother initially wanted him to have no part of football, he kept coming to practice. His commitment to succeed despite these obstacles continues to inspire me to this day.

We all set up roadblocks and give ourselves excuses why we cannot accomplish something. When obstacles stand in your way, instead of focusing on the problem, focus on the solution. Smitty had low self-esteem thanks to his speech impediment. It would have been so easy for him to play the victim. Instead, this young man found a solution to his problem simply by joining a team. There *really* is a solution to every problem. What's yours?

*Opportunities multiply as they are seized.*

-Sun Tzu

# Jumping in With Both Feet

I travel to Mexico every year with my family and a couple of our friends in tow. We always stay at an all-inclusive resort so that food is easy to get when someone gets hungry, which seems to happen continually. Every morning after our workout we find a central location right by the main pool so we can join in all the activities and easily recruit for our favorite pastime: beach volleyball.

I am not sure if the entire family agrees, but I think it is the most important event of our trip, one that each member of the family participates in. With four of us being over 6' 1" and my wife Karen being a pretty consistent player, we are a competitive group. We like to call ourselves "Team Canada."

It still amazes me that after 20 years of going down to these resorts, most of the beach volleyball courts stay empty until someone picks up a ball and walks around recruiting people to make up two teams. I usually take on the role of the recruiter, due largely to my inability to sit still for more than a minute. It's easy to get people to participate in the game and, pretty soon, everyone is having a blast and there is a line-up of new people wanting to join in. Last year, we even recruited some players who happened to be from Red Deer.

They weren't even staying at our resort, but – given their height and skill level – we eagerly welcomed them aboard Team Canada. Most of the people who joined weren't novices – they have played volleyball at some point in their lives. However, our last trip was a little different. I approached a couple with a teenage daughter about playing some beach volleyball with us. Both the husband and wife kindly declined, but their daughter jumped up and said she would love to play.

At this point, her parents looked at her and reminded her that she didn't know how to play volleyball.

"How else will I learn if I don't try?" she replied.

I told the parents that I would take care of their daughter so they should not worry. I'm not sure if they were more concerned with her trying her hand at volleyball for the first time, or frightened that a big bald Sasquatch like me, whom they had only met for 10 seconds, told them he would "take care" of their teenage daughter. However, Alex - that was the girl's name - readily jumped up and followed me onto the volleyball court. She knew nothing about this game and struggled quite a bit at first. There came a point where I thought she was going to quit and just go back to tanning. I decided to improve my "on the job" training, or we risked losing Alex. So I pulled her aside for a bit and got a couple of our teammates to help her out. They did a good job because Alex started to get better. Teammates were high-fiving her and her confidence improved with each game. Once she started getting the hang of it, you couldn't wipe the smile off her face. Over the next couple of days, when I started walking down the beach to recruit new blood, Alex was already waiting at the court.

After supper one night, I was approached by Alex's parents, who wanted to thank me for helping their daughter out on the volleyball court. I told them it was a pleasure and that I had enjoyed watching Alex's progress.

"You know, she is quite different from us," Alex's mother said.

I didn't know what she meant by that comment and whether or not I'd be walking on thin ice if I responded. So, I simply asked Alex's mom what made her daughter different.

She went on to explain that they had raised two children and, once both left the house, the parents decided to adopt Alex from Russia. Alex was already a teenager when they brought her back to the United States to start her new life.

It was a bit odd how Alex was eager to learn new things, while her parents preferred to watch – rather than participate in – the events going on around them. I had chatted quite a bit with Alex over the week. She told me that when she came to the United States, she could not believe how many opportunities were available there. However, she also mentioned that she couldn't understand how so many people failed to take advantage of all those chances. I found these comments very interesting, especially since they came from a 14 year-old girl. It was wonderful to see how enthusiastically she joined our volleyball team, despite never having played the game before. She wanted to learn and jumped in with both feet (no pun intended), wore a smile on her face, and ended up loving the game.

## GET COMFORTABLE BEING UNCOMFORTABLE

All of this happened because this young girl, who was raised in a more restrictive culture, happily embraced new opportunities and made the best of them.

Alex made me think about all the opportunities that come our way that we fail to seize out of fear, or because we allow others to tell us what we should or should not do. Maybe it's time I head back to Russia to remind myself how good we all have it here. Do you take advantage of every opportunity that comes your way?

*Success is achieved by developing our strengths,
not by eliminating our weaknesses.*

-Marilyn vos Savant

# The Report Card

Growing up in Saskatoon, I had a friend named Matthew. He was a smart kid and, for the most part, stayed out of trouble. Everyone was always amazed at how beautifully he could draw. He captivated his classmates as he drew caricatures of them. Everyone thought he was the most gifted person in the entire school. I remember struggling while drawing something as simple as two stick people, so I was truly astounded by his artistic talent.

Matthew was usually upbeat, but one particular morning, his head was down and he made no attempt to make eye contact or strike up conversation. I knew something was wrong. I walked over to him and asked if he was okay. When he looked up, I noticed that his face was swollen. His eyes were red and you could tell that he had been crying very recently.

Matthew explained that his report card had come home and his dad didn't think much of his grades. His dad expressed his displeasure by laying one helluva beating on him. I was absolutely stunned. I asked him how his parents could be upset about his grades – sure, he struggled in math, but all his other marks were decent.

Later in life I learned about the "Report Card Theory."

According to research done by the Novokowsky Consulting Group, the majority of people first notice the lowest mark on a report card and respond to it. In Matthew's case, his parents focused on the 'D' he got in mathematics, while ignoring the better grades he had in other subjects.

Outside the extreme reaction of his father, Matthew's folks were not that different from other people. Their focus went towards motivating their son to improve his 'D' in mathematics. The Novokowsky research shows that it's likely the lowest mark will increase in a scenario like this. After all, there's always room for improvement. What's more interesting though, is what happens to the other grades. The majority of the time, a high grade such as an 'A' will drop on the next report card because it's difficult to maintain consistently high grades in all subjects.

I truly believe that everyone has a gift in life. Everyone has their 'A' subject. Matthew's 'A' subject happened to be art. Research shows that if you focus on a person's 'A' subject, and provide encouragement to them about the subject (such as telling them how amazing they are in that field), their 'A' will actually turn into an A+. Even more surprisingly, their 'D' will normally increase as a direct result of the higher confidence level of the individual.

After finishing university, I actually ran into Matthew in Calgary. He informed me he had opened up his own custom art shop and that business was very good!

Whether you're a parent, coach, teacher or manager, there's something to be learned from this story. Do you tend to focus on the

## GET COMFORTABLE BEING UNCOMFORTABLE

'D's' or the 'A's'? Studies show that you will have better students, colleagues and family members when you focus on their excellence rather than their failures.

What are your 'A's'? Isn't it time to focus on them?

*Don't walk behind me; I may not lead. Don't walk in front of me;
I may not follow. Just walk beside me and be my friend.*

-Albert Camus

# Beside Each Other

Throughout my professional football career, Steve Rodehutskors was my teammate and best friend. He was also the best man at my wedding.

Much like me, Steve was a dreamer. He had goals and he wasn't afraid to aim high. From the time he was a teenager, Steve dreamed of not only winning a Grey Cup ring, but also to establish a career in veterinary medicine.

I first met Steve at the beginning of the 1987 Blue Bombers training camp. He was a big farm boy from Strathmore, Alberta. He had played basketball, and not football, most of his life. He went to the University of Lethbridge to play basketball and played in the National Championship. Then he transferred to the University of Calgary after his second year to give football a try. He ended up playing on the Vanier Cup winning football team with the University of Calgary.

His athletic success was remarkable. Few people can start at one university, in one sport, transfer to another to try their hand in another sport, and achieve outstanding success in both. What is even more incredible is that Steve did this while taking a full load of science classes and maintaining straight A's. But, as I said, Steve never had a problem travelling the road that no one else wanted to take.

I didn't have an ideal start to the 1988 season with the Winnipeg Blue Bombers. I injured my knee during an exhibition game, had major surgery, and was forced to miss all 18 regular season games. During my rehab, my starting position on the offensive line was filled by none other than Steve. As devastating as the injury was, the fact that it opened an opportunity for Steve somehow lessened the sting. He gained experience, proved his abilities, and became a full-time starter in the Canadian Football League. I'm glad I could help!

When CFL players are on the road, they all have their own pre-game rituals. Some go out for a big supper. Others stay in their room and play crib or watch TV. Of course, some rituals involve sneaking out past curfew to check out the nightlife!

Steve and I had a routine that was totally our own. On the afternoon before game day, there was always a team meeting. After the team meeting, Steve and I would scour the city for a restaurant or bar that had a trivia game. Steve loved to flex his mental muscles every bit as much as he enjoyed punishing opponents on the football grid. It seemed like Steve could rattle off the answer to just about any question before it was even displayed on the screen. Sometimes, Steve would let me enter in the answers on the electronic keyboard so I could look like the genius in front of the other patrons. Nine times out of ten we would have the highest score and win some tacky prize or another.

Once we'd filled our bellies and played several rounds of trivia, we'd typically go find a book store to find something to read. While

## GET COMFORTABLE BEING UNCOMFORTABLE

I leafed my way through magazine titles such as *Sports Illustrated,* Steve would bury his nose in the latest books about his greatest passion: medicine.

About a week before our first playoff game in 1988, my knee was evaluated by our team doctor. I was cleared to play in the playoffs. Whose spot would I take? You guessed it – Steve's. Talk about an awkward situation. Replacing the guy you share your hopes and dreams with every day just as his journey towards a Grey Cup was about to get underway. For the first time ever, I had no idea what to say to him. Steve had to have been bitter, but his only words were those of encouragement.

We won our first playoff game by the slimmest of margins. Steve stood on the sidelines, a little quieter than usual, but full of support. In our second game against Toronto, our All-Pro lineman, Chris Walby went down with an injury. Chris was our Right Tackle, and played right beside me on the offensive line. Guess what? My best man was back! He replaced Chris Walby and we played side-by-side for the rest of the victory against Toronto, paving our way to the Grey Cup Championship game.

One week later, Steve and I played beside each other again, this time in the biggest game of our lives. We couldn't wipe the smiles off of our faces. The first time Steve and I played beside one another for an entire game was the 76th Grey Cup in Ottawa. What a stage to be on together. If you're old enough to remember, the Blue Bombers won that game in the closest Grey Cup in history, with a final score of 22-21. Both Steve and I had realized our boyhood dreams.

We hugged each other as the final gun went off. We were not sure if the fans were comfortable seeing two sweaty men, weighing close to 275lbs, standing in the middle of the field hugging each other, but it seemed perfectly natural to us. We went to the locker room to celebrate, only to find the place packed with media, wives, girlfriends, and fans. We asked for a couple of bottles of Champagne and meandered out to centre field. Before we knew it, fans and teammates joined our party.

These memories were caught on film. Up until recently, CBC still played our centre field celebration now and again, usually during its Grey Cup broadcasts.

After football, Steve did indeed achieve his second goal. He got his degree in veterinary medicine and moved back to his home town of Strathmore and became a veterinarian. Through hard work, dedication and perseverance, Steve achieved both of his goals. He was challenged many times along the way, but he stayed the course and took those challenges in stride. When faced with unexpected obstacles, he just kept working hard and was rewarded with joyful and exciting accomplishments.

Years after our Grey Cup victories, Steve and I were side-by-side again. I recited the story you just read to Steve at his bedside in October 2007. Realizing all he had accomplished brought a smile to a face that only had hours to live. Steve died later that day, succumbing to cancer at the age of 43.

We can't control how long each of us has on this earth. But we can control the life we lead while we're here. In your final days, will you be thinking about what could have been? Or, will you be like my friend Steve – beaming with pride about a life well-lived. The choice is yours. Maybe it's time to write down a few goals that will bring a smile to your face?

# Acknowledgments

I would like to express my deepest appreciation to the entire Fast Track team, particularly David Wilson and Jenny Lawrence. David, your ability to bring life to my stories through your editing was truly amazing. You're a young man with a very bright future. Jenny, you did much more than make this book look beautiful with your design work, you were the glue that kept the team together. Special thanks to Dave Dubeau for your guidance throughout the project. And to Darren Weeks: thank you for making me uncomfortable and giving me the push I needed to write this book. Finally, to my wife Karen, thanks for all your help making sense of my random thoughts.

# About Bob Molle

Bob Molle is one of the world's leading experts on goal-setting and personal achievement. He is the only man to ever win an Olympic Medal and a Grey Cup Championship. In addition to helping people from all walks of life, Bob has worked with major sales, marketing, financial and health organizations. By sharing his unique approach to goal-setting, he has inspired thousands of people to reach their full potential and better their lives. Bob is also an internationally renowned motivational speaker. For more information about Bob, visit www.bobmolle.com. To book Bob for your next speaking engagement please email bookings@emjmarketing.com

Free audio download for readers of
*Get Comfortable Being Uncomfortable*

To help reach your full potential, you can now listen to Improving Your Performance, one of Bob's most popular audio programs (retail value $46.95). In this unique, inspiring and powerful presentation you will learn new ideas that will help fast track your journey to happiness. Simply visit www.bobmolle.com, sign up for your free newsletter and download your copy. I encourage you to share this information with your family, friends and colleagues.